STOR IE
and
MIRACLES

igloo

The First Miracle

John 2

One day, Jesus was invited to a wedding. The marriage was to take place in Galilee, in a town called Cana. Jesus's mother, Mary, was invited too.

Everyone enjoyed themselves but, half way through the wedding feast, the wine ran out.

"What are we to do?" asked the Master of the Feast. "How can we enjoy the rest of our food without wine?"

Mary overheard the worried man and thought Jesus might be able to do something about it. She whispered into her son's ear. "Can you help? This poor man has run out of wine to offer his guests."

"Do not ask me this," Jesus replied anxiously. "My time has not yet come."

But Mary was already turning to the servants, saying, "Do whatever he tells you to do."

Not wishing to disobey his mother, Jesus decided to help.

Nearby lay six empty water jars, from which the wedding guests had washed their hands before eating. Jesus told the servants to refill all six of the jars with water.

"Now," he said, "pour a little of the water into a cup and take it to the Master of the Feast."

The servants did as they were told.

When the Master of the Feast tasted the water, it had miraculously turned into wine.

"What wonderful wine! What a clever man you are!" he exclaimed, slapping the bridegroom on the back. "Everyone else serves the best wine first and keeps the cheapest until last. But you have saved the best until last!"

Only the servants who served the wine knew of Jesus's powers. This was the first miracle that Jesus ever performed.

Jesus Heals the Sick

Matthew 8, Luke 7, 18

As Jesus's fame grew and grew, more people flocked to his side, hoping to catch a glimpse of him. The ill and diseased fought their way through the crowds, hoping that Jesus would heal them.

One day a blind beggar, unable to push his way to Jesus's side, shouted out:
"Son of David, have mercy on me!"
Jesus heard the blind man's call and asked that he be brought to him.
"What do you want from me?" Jesus asked.
"Lord, let me see!" pleaded the beggar.
Jesus laid his hands on the man's head, and said:
"Receive your sight. Your faith has healed you."
When Jesus took his hands away, the beggar could see again.

Another time, Jesus was asked to visit the house of a Roman soldier. The soldier's servant was very ill and close to death.
As Jesus neared his house, the soldier rushed out to meet him.

"Lord, although I am not worthy to have you enter my home, please say a prayer so my servant will be healed."
Jesus was surprised and moved by the strength of the soldier's belief in him.
"I have not seen faith as strong as this in the whole of Israel," he said.

After Jesus had left him, the soldier went back into his house and found his servant completely cured of his illness.

Walking on Water

Matthew 14, Mark 6, John 6

After Jesus had finished speaking one afternoon, he told his disciples to sail home in their boats. He told them he wanted to go into the hills and pray, and he would meet with them later.

But as the disciples made their way out to sea, the wind grew strong and it began to rain. The further they sailed from the shore, the worse the weather became. The wind howled, the driving rain lashed at their faces and huge waves rolled and crashed around them.

The disciples became very afraid. They didn't know if they were going to keep the boat from sinking. The worst thing of all was that it would soon be dark.

It took all the disciples' strength to keep the little boat afloat. They worked hard all night knowing that they would surely drown if they failed.

As the sun started to rise, the disciples were very weary from all their efforts.
Suddenly, they all cried out in terror, when out of the early morning mist, a ghostly figure appeared to be walking on the water towards them. But the figure calmed them, simply saying:
"Do not be afraid. It is I, Jesus."

Peter could not believe his eyes and shouted out:
"If it is really you, Lord. Command me to walk on the water as well!" Jesus held out his hand. "Come," he said.
Peter scrambled over the side of the boat and tried to walk on the water too, but courage failed him and he began to sink.
"Lord, save me!" he shouted.

Jesus grasped his hand tightly, and helped him back to the safety of the small boat.
"Peter," said Jesus gently. "How little your faith is. Why did you doubt me?"
Peter asked for Jesus's forgiveness, and then he and the other disciples knelt down in front of him.
"You really are the Son of God," they said.

Jairus's Daughter

Matthew 9, Mark5, Luke 8

There was once a man called Jairus who was the leader of a synagogue. One day, while Jesus was preaching, Jairus pushed his way through the crowds to see him.

"Help me, Master," he said. "My little daughter is very ill. I'm afraid she's going to die. Please come to my house and see her."

Jesus agreed at once. He and Jairus began to make their way through the throngs of people that now followed Jesus everywhere.

When a woman touched Jesus's robe as he passed by, Jesus turned and asked, "Who touched me?"

The woman stepped forward.

"I did, Master. I have been ill for many years. Now that I have touched your robe, I am healed."

"Your faith has made you well," said Jesus. "Go in peace."

A messenger from Jairus's house was sent out to meet them.
"I have bad news for you, Jairus," he said. "Your daughter has died."
Jairus fell to the ground with grief.

At Jairus's house, many people were standing outside weeping. Jesus comforted them.

"The girl is not dead. She is just sleeping," he said.

Jesus went to the girl's side and took her hand.

"Get up, my child," he said, softly.

The girl slowly opened her eyes and then climbed out of bed as Jesus had commanded. She was completely cured.

Feeding the Five Thousand

Matthew 14, Mark 6, Luke 9, John 6

One day, Jesus was speaking on a hillside near to the shores of Lake Galilee. Over five thousand people had come to hear his words. By the evening everyone was still there, listening intently to what he had to say.

One of his disciples rushed up to him.
"Lord, these people have been here all day with nothing to eat. They must be very hungry, and all I can find is a small boy who has five loaves of bread and two fishes."
"Bring him to me," said Jesus.
When the boy arrived, Jesus took the basket of loaves and fishes from him and bowed his head in prayer.
Jesus then began to walk among the people, handing out the food.

Magically, the small basket of loaves and fishes never seemed to run out. Eventually, all five thousand people had been fed until they could eat no more. There was even enough food left over to fill twelve large baskets.

Jesus Raises the Dead

Luke 10, John 11

When Jesus was in Jerusalem, he often stayed with his friends, Mary, Martha and their brother, Lazarus.

Once, while Jesus was teaching outside the city, Mary sent a message to him telling him that her brother, Lazarus, was very ill. She wanted Jesus to go to Lazarus and make him well again.

But, when Jesus arrived two days later, Lazarus had already died.
"Lord, if you had arrived earlier, my brother would still be alive!" Martha cried.
"Lazarus will live again," said Jesus. "Take me to him."
Lazarus's body had been placed in a large cave, and a huge rock had been put in front of its entrance.
Jesus asked that the rock be moved away.
When the rock had been moved, all was quiet except for a light breeze rattling the leaves in the trees.
Then Jesus spoke:
"Lazarus, come out!" he commanded.

Everyone gasped, when Lazarus stumbled out of the tomb, still wrapped in his grave clothes.

"Our brother is alive!" wept Mary and Martha, who got down on their knees and gave their thanks to God.

This was one of Jesus's greatest miracles. After hearing of the raising of Lazarus, many more people realized that Jesus was the true Son of God. But there were other people who were afraid of Jesus's powers and wanted to destroy him. Jesus knew that his time on Earth would be short and, that eventually, he would suffer and die.

The Paralysed Man

Matthew 9, Mark 2, Luke 5

Once, Jesus was teaching inside someone's house. As usual, there were hundreds of people who wanted to get close to him and hear what he was saying. The house quickly filled up with many people, and there were lots more outside, crowding around the door and windows hoping to get a glimpse of him.

Suddenly, four men approached the house. They were carrying their friend on a bed mat. He had suffered a terrible disease that had left him paralyzed. His friends were taking him to see Jesus, whom they hoped would help. But, there were so many people crowding around the door, it was impossible to get through.

One of the men had an idea.
"Why don't we cut a hole in the roof," he said. "It's only made of straw. Then we can lower our friend into the room where Jesus is."

The others agreed and, soon, the paralyzed man was lying at Jesus's feet.